The Harvest

The Harvest

Merci L. McKinley

I2E

Inspiration2Empower Press

The Harvest

Published by Inspiration2Empower Press ™

Copyright © 2017 by Merci L. McKinley

Published by:

Inspiration2empower Press

Editor:

Merci L. McKinley

www.upliftpublications.com

Publishing consultant:

Professional Woman Publishing, LLC

www.pwnbooks.com

Cover Design:

blazingcovers@gmail.com

For more information about special discounts for bulk purchases, please contact

Merci L. McKinley at www.upliftpublications.com

ISBN: 978-0-692-87145-4

Library of Congress Number: 2017905251

Printed in the United States of America

TABLE OF CONTENTS

FOREWORD

"The Harvest' is a manifesto of Christian womanhood that celebrates the faith and resilience we all have as children of God and the power we hold within us as His daughters to survive, overcome, grow and transcend in any circumstance. It's a must read!"

–Ambassador Dr. Margaret Dureke, President & CEO, WETATi, Margaretspeaks.com & author of "How to Succeed Against All Odds!"

ACKNOWLEDGEMENT

I would like to thank God, His Son, Jesus Christ and the Holy Spirit, for their unconditional love and support. They have never forsaken me. I thank God for allowing me to experience not worldly love, but love filled with spiritual balance through rebirth in Christ. I also thank God for sacrificing His Son, Jesus Christ, so we can all have life more abundantly. Jesus is The Bread of Life that can neither be defined nor taken away by man.

Thank you, to my family, especially my parents and grand-mothers who made sure I had seeds of faith planted within me. To my mother, who gifted me with the Bible when I was in fourth grade, I give an abundance of gratitude. It is this gift that directed me, time and time again, to the Almighty, Merciful God. That Bible sustained me through my many trials and tribulations. There are simply no words to express my overwhelming gratitude.

INTRODUCTION

Why I Wrote the Harvest

I lived in shame which led me to hide the full extent of what I suffered. I hid it quite well. In hiding, I wasn't living. I would wake up by the grace of God each day, but I wasn't thriving. I placed myself inside a box, both mentally and emotionally. By now, you're probably saying to yourself this is no way to live. I know there are others who are still living the same way. Through my praying to God, I realized none of us were born inside a box. It's our way of thinking that places us there. The stronger I grew in my faith, the more I understood the box didn't exist. The courage to speak comes from recognizing it was God who kept me and He will continue to sustain me. In my denial and cover-up, I had only God to rely upon. I prayed as if my life depended upon it, because quite often it did.

I searched for answers and a sense of fulfillment. I looked to man to provide the answers. I found unhealthy ways to provide fulfillment and validation. I was overwhelmed with unhealthy feelings when I reflected on my past:

Abandonment--because of my biological mother.

Uncleanliness--because of being molested while growing up.

Unworthiness--because of suffering sexual trauma in the military.

Unloved—because of a physically abusive romantic relationship.

I cried out to God, desperately needing Him to breathe life back into my existence. I was a shell of a person; walking amongst the living. Yet, though I walked, I wasn't truly living. When I cried out, he listened. When I cried out, he answered. I simply had to let go, and let God. I had to let God do the mending. It no longer became a matter of why, but more of how. I lost years of my life due to trauma. When one storm came, another surely followed. For years, my life was this vicious cycle. I carried burdens and bore crosses. In God, I learned some crosses are not mine to bear. The burdens I carried were not mine to own. God lifted those burdens. I just had to learn how to allow Him to lift those burdens. Oftentimes, when we desperately want to release ourselves from our burdens, we don't know how. Out of habit, we pick these burdens up again.

I was so guilty of these very same habits. Until I had to allow God to show me the way, break the habit, and never return to it God blessed me with my grandmothers and my mother. They understood the importance of Proverbs 22:6 KJV "Train up a child in the way he should go: and when he is old, he will not depart from it." God allowed them to give me the gift of learning how to have a relationship with Him for myself. I am a firm believer that sometimes we die before our time. Physically, I didn't perish, but mentally, emotionally and spiritually, I did. It was a struggle to not let my faith be taken by circumstances. It was a struggle, but my God; our God fought for me. Tears that once flowed from brokenness, flowed from wholeness. Tears that once flowed from hurt not yet spoken, flowed from a voice that has risen. If God can do this for me, He can do the same for you.

I know what it's like to weather the storms of life. I know what it's like to question my existence. I know what it's like to be brought to my knees and struggle to increase my faith. As a student of life, I know of many things and travel the journey of life with you. There are questions that burn within us and we seek answers. They can only be gathered from our spiritual walk and Christian faith. How can we continue to claim the answers to our questions and grow in strength? How can we stand upright physically and move beyond being wounded mentally? How can we truly stand upright in God and with God? In The Harvest, my personal testimony will show that with God, it is very much possible. We are born into this world, but we must be born again in Jesus Christ. In His love, we can always perform to our fullest abilities. I don't profess to have a "one-size-fits-all" answer, but I know God will ultimately provide answers to each of us.

My why is to present a gift before you. As you read "The Harvest," my hope is to propel you forward into your Christian walk. My hope is for you to embrace the same gift I was given and allow God to do the mending!

CHAPTER 1

A Testimony

*"Other people are going to find healing in your wounds. Your
greatest life message and your most effective ministry will come out of
your deepest hurts."*

–Rick Warren

I heard that God gives us a testimony for certain reasons. The testimony is not for us to keep within ourselves, but to share with others. As Christian women, we are called to teach. Like Jonah, sometimes we attempt to escape or reason ourselves out of His call to teach and to minister. Sometimes, we think because of our past transgressions, we are not qualified to testify. God often calls the unqualified to do the work only He can accomplish through them. I'm not a pastor, but merely called to testify. When God calls us, we must listen in order to serve a greater need beyond ourselves. I humbly answered that call because I know someone needs to hear what has been placed within me to speak. My testimony is already many pages, as He has allowed, with more chapters of my life to come.

There are several chapters that give you a brief insight into my testimony; it is where you will find my true voice. For years, I wore a mask to please others. I concealed myself through academic overachievement, hiding my true value and worth. While hiding, I expended unnecessary energy maintaining illusions to please others.

In wearing those masks, my relationship with God was not only affected but renewed at the same time. What becomes of the little girl who discovers she was abandoned at birth by her biological mother? What becomes of the young woman who experienced sexual abuse during several episodes of her life growing up, serving in the military, and domestic violence? She rose in Christ with the unconditional love of an all-merciful God. She rose to let others know that they, too, can be provided the same if they deeply plow their soil with His seeds. It wasn't an easy journey, as I had to face truths and commit to the process in action.

I lived in shame which led me to hide the full extent of what I've suffered through. I hid it quite well. When I consider the years I lost due to trauma, I know it was God who allowed me to even make it this far. I would cry out, asking Him to please don't let me leave this earth without having lived. You see, I never knew quite how to live. I never knew how to develop who Merci ultimately was. As children we are given the tools to learn and develop this for ourselves. I was given the tools by my grandmother and mother. Yet, these very same tools disappeared. My innocence, my childhood was taken away by a relative. It was a relative who stole my voice, my laughter, and my esteem. I was molested from the age of five to nine. My young mind could not process what was happening to me. My body reminded me of it every time it burned when I went to pee.

I maintained appearances as long as I was able. I couldn't share my true thoughts with family or friends. Inwardly, I suffered because I hadn't found the words to fully broadcast my loss. In God, I developed my voice. That same voice has allowed me to liberate myself, acknowledging my depression. I was not left unscathed by my trauma. Early on, I was determined not to become a statistic of my prior experiences. I kept the secret as long as I could. I didn't want to give my family reasons to regret adopting me.

Growing up, I watched all kinds of Lifetime movies, documentaries, and shows similar to A&E Intervention Series. Since I didn't lead a life of full addiction or spiral completely out of control, I thought I was somehow unscathed. That was false in every sense of word. I lived with bouts of depression built by fear and the broken pieces left in the aftermath of molestation. I feared how my thoughts would be received by others. Through God, we must learn that fear only serves with the purpose we give it.

Surely a person who appears to have it all together would be frowned upon, once the truth was revealed. My negative thoughts became my reality. These thoughts engulfed me like a tidal wave. While I physically can't swim, God allowed me to learn how to spiritually swim. Each time I wanted to reach out to others, I would think my way out of it. I believed no one would have empathy for me. I was sinking within my thoughts. Yet, It was God whom allowed me to stay afloat.

I was brought to my knees, questioning God in every way possible. Just as Moses would question God, as he would witness and endure suffering. Numbers 11:11 KJV "And Moses said unto the Lord, wherefore hast thou afflicted thy servant? And wherefore have I not found favor in thy sight, that thou layest the burden of all this people upon me?" I carried the burden of reliving my afflictions. Not only did I question God's existence, but I questioned His love for me. When I was growing up, my grandmother gave me a book titled "My Book of Bible Stories." I read it because I loved to read and quite frankly, reading was my escape.

I remember Jonah's story. Jonah was stubborn, but called by God to preach to Nineveh. Many times over, he questioned God and many times over God answered him. God specifically chose

Jonah to deliver the city from destruction. Originally, Jonah chose to flee from His calling. He bought passage on a ship at the seaport to escape from God. A storm threatened to sink the ship. To save the crew and the vessel of his escape, Jonah volunteered to be cast overboard, and was swallowed by a whale. In the whale's belly, Jonah cried out to God, the very same God he desperately tried to avoid. God answered Jonah's disobedience with deliverance. What could a stubborn man have that God would want to show others? He too answered my disobedience with deliverance. As hard as my grandmothers fought to sow seeds of faith in me, I met them with disobedience. I repelled those seeds as surely God did not love me. Surely God did not exist in the midst of my molestation. Surely God did not exist in the many trials and tribulations I'd endured. The more I grew in my faith, the more I realized my thinking was completely false.

Who would have thought my grandmother's gift would be relevant in my life's journey? I was only a little girl when I received that book and my first Bible from my mother. My mother saw fit to give me a Bible in the 4th grade as a gift for making straight A's in school. It is no coincidence that certain things in my life would lead me back to these gifts. It most certainly is not coincidence these very same gifts would become my refuge. These very same gifts would become my escape. I didn't have a clue of what I was reading but as I grew, I still read. Only when I matured, did these gifts take on a new meaning.

There is a difference between grew and matured. We can grow by way of age, but we mature in the wisdom acquired. The wisdom acquired through God is what gives us the right to say we have truly matured. Looking back, God was always with me, but at times I never felt Him near. I would pray, but did not know if I was praying the right prayer. My mother would tell me during church service, you could hear the barrettes in my hair clacking together.

It was because every time the preacher would say "Mercy," I thought he was calling me. My head would turn every which way. I would say "Momma, he is calling my name." I would observe members of the congregation catching the "Holy Ghost", after praying. It was as if God was speaking directly to them. So naturally, I thought because I wasn't catching the "Holy Ghost", I wasn't praying right. I expected this each time I would return to the church during my trials and tribulations. Is there such a thing as the right prayer and how to truly pray? I was filled with questions.

I have come to believe that God is an intentional God. He intentionally sent His son, Jesus Christ, to die on the cross for our sins. He is intentional in the rearranging of our lives to get our attention. Growing up, I was overweight. I ate constantly. I ate to build a wall between myself and others. I ate to keep from being hurt. Food provided comfort. I was not prepared for how my body reacted. Naturally, I was very self-conscious about my appearance. When we would take our trips to New Orleans, I thought my family were making fun of my weight. My aunt, also my godmother, would make me feel even more self-conscious with her laughter. I was overly sensitive. We rarely kept in touch as I got older.

While stationed at Fort Hood, TX, I didn't receive the call, but rather a word through social media--my aunt had a fourth stroke. Without any hesitation, I went to be by her bedside. Deep within, I harbored certain feelings of anger towards my aunt. When I arrived and saw her lying there with the machines and tubes, I was over- whelmed. I didn't let this show as I prayed inwardly. I felt helpless. I didn't know anything else but to pray. Every weekend, I would travel from Killeen to Dallas, to be at her bedside. One weekend, I decided to make a playlist of inspirational music and gospel songs. When I got to the hospital, I placed the headphones in her ears and sat. I would watch her monitors, and stay on the hospital staff to make sure she was given quality care. I didn't rest. I was afraid to doze off and miss reminding the on call staff that she needed to be rotated. I couldn't do that by myself, but I assisted the nurses to make sure it was done correctly. As soon as I would get on the highway, I would worry. When I'm worrying, I cannot rest. I worried so much, I felt I was going to have a stroke, too.

For weeks, I did not rest. I had not read my Bible in a very long time. One night, I pulled out my Bible given to me by my father, to replace the one I lost in Iraq. I turned to Philippians 4:6-7 KJV 6 "Be careful for nothing; but in everything by prayer and supplication with thanksgiving let your requests be made known unto God." 7 "And the peace of God, which passeth all understanding, shall keep your hearts and minds through Christ Jesus." My heart was still troubled, but I tried to get some rest. When I am close in my faith in God, He speaks to me through my dreams. Imagine my reaction when I rose the next morning, realizing I received a vision in my dreams. It had been a very long time since I felt the presence of God within my dreams.

In my dream, I was in a dark place trying to flee. Everywhere I turned, I was being approached by a circle of figures in white. I could not identify them and I was frantically trying to escape. As the figures drew nearer, I saw a hand stretched out from above commanding me to yield. I yielded under the outstretched hand from above. I woke up the next morning and immediately checked on my aunt. She showed enough improvement to be moved from the hospital to a rehabilitation facility. When Mother's Day weekend came, I went to see her. Although she could not speak, she was trying to smile, while attempting movement. My aunt's nurse came in and asked if we were mothers. My aunt, with all her available strength, lifted her hand and pointed at me. I thought that was odd since she knew I was not a mother. As the day went on, I realized it was her acknowledgement of my presence. She knew I was there, by her bedside, in her most difficult hour. It was God that allowed me to be there. It was God that allowed me to put aside the differences I was struggling with and be there for her.

My time in the military took its toll on my body, resulting in multiple surgeries. My inherited ailments also resulted in several surgeries. Since I was in Texas, my family was not able to be with me during those moments. Again, I harbored resentment as they could have found a way to be there. When my aunt had her strokes, her room was filled with family. They traveled from near and far, to be with her. God removed my resentment. He spoke to me and settled the thoughts I had gathered over the years. Being adopted, I always felt like I was treated differently. They say blood is thicker than water. Negative thoughts plagued me for years that their blood didn't flow through my veins. Maybe, that's why they were not at my side. Maybe, that's why the phone calls were sporadic while I was recovering and rehabilitating. When my aunt stretched her hand towards me at the nurse question, God spoke to me. He was pleading with me and my conscience.

When I got to my car, after leaving my aunt, I pulled my Bible from the glove compartment. I was rebellious, still wrestling with my burdens. I thought my burdens fueled my inner drive. I had lived with my burdens for years. Each time I thought of my biological mother, I would work ten times harder to prove to myself I was worthy. In hindsight, it was my way of showing her I was worthy. God instructed me to release my burdens. He was speaking through others and their situations. Yet, these very same burdens I carried were a part of me and they were hard to release. You would have thought I'd welcome a chance to drop my burdens. The problem was I didn't know how. Just a few months later, the reasons why God pleaded with me through that moment would be revealed.

Somewhere, I read a blog that said your life is to be lived with respect to your origins. It must be lived with the greatest courage to love yourself enough to move forward. This can be a difficult process for some to go through, especially through the feeling of brokenness. For me, it definitely was. I penned these words because I never thought I would be a survivor of domestic violence. In reflection, God was trying to teach me boundaries and discernment over the years. Unresolved issues can lead to a never ending cycle of searching for satisfaction in man versus being fulfilled in God.

Unresolved past issues can cause us to become prey to others. Speaking of those issues to the person preying can place someone within inches of their life. I knew my abuser through years of casual encounters. Every so often, he would reappear in my life. My abuser was relentless and very methodical. He was controlling and manipulative. I never knew this, until his final return to my life, a few months after I'd been caring for my aunt. He wanted to move way too fast, but I still wouldn't fully submit to his pace. Just weeks prior, I'd asked God to reveal to me who this man really was—his true personality. Sometimes, when the answers don't come immediately, we think God does not hear us. God had been revealing to me over the years how my abuser was, but I did not take heed. My abuser was leading a double life.

The ability of discernment God was placing within me, was met with consequence. My consequence was a violent rage, piercing of my self-esteem and hearing of my abuser's suicidal thoughts. In his alcoholic rage, he choked me one night outside of my residence. The look within his eyes and the satisfaction from it was frightening. For days I was left with swelling in my neck. I had difficulty swallowing, eating and speaking. The weeks that followed would add further insult to injury. I was beaten in ways that left me physically scarred. I'll never forget his laughter or his actions in the process. It was this same laughter that played in my mind during my recovery. Only by God's Grace am I still here. I underwent surgery to repair additional damage from that beating. At a very young age, I had to undergo a total knee replacement.

Years in the military, rucking over uneven terrain for miles on end with 45 lbs. on my back took its toll on my knee. After that day I was beaten, my knee needed more revising surgery. My abuser had laughed with a sense of pride as he'd struck and kicked the metal implant. As a result, the metal implant loosened. I remember waking up from surgery, feeling broken inside. Surprising those that knew me, I showed them I still had will and motivation. Some of my doctors said, "Time is of the essence, your rehabilitation depends on it." I willed myself, with all my might, to lift my leg and perform the exercises. I could not perform the exercises. When they left, I cried to God, "Please, help me, father. I can't do this. Do you hear me? Where are you? Please, don't leave me, father?" He said we can always turn to Him. Matthew 11:28-30 KJV "28: Come unto me, all ye that labour and are heavy laden, and I will give you rest. 29: Take my yoke upon you, and learn of me; for I am meek and lowly in heart: and ye shall find rest unto your souls. 30: For my yoke is easy, and my burden is light"

I would take to the walker with as much strength as I possibly could. I would pray, "Father, please order my steps." Learning how to walk again was a painful test. Assuredly, it was none other than God that made it possible for me to walk again. Each step I took in rehab, I asked myself, "How did I get here?" By now, I was medically retired from the service, but not without combat-related Post Traumatic Stress Disorder (PTSD), sexual trauma, domestic violence and other ailments. I never imagined myself a disabled veteran when I transitioned from service to civilian.

By the time Domestic Violence Awareness Month (October) had come, I found myself participating in a social media forum. A question addressed to the forum was," Who all are survivors?" I boldly answered, "I am a survivor." Although I knew in my heart I was not truly healed, I responded. It's said when you tell your story without tears, you've healed. I set out to do the video without tears, but they appeared just as freely. With conviction, I spoke into the webcam to give His words. I pleaded to anyone watching and said, "I wouldn't wish this on anyone, and that you have to leave. I wouldn't want anyone to walk a mile in my shoes." I released the video, and shared it within the forum as instructed. Within minutes after it ended, women spoke up and said, "Merci, you saved my life." I was nervous, as I didn't heed to my sense of embarrassment. I just wanted to change some other woman's life--someone on the other side of that webcam.

I have that webcam's power, manifested tenfold, through "The Harvest." I wanted to share this to empower you to live life progressively through Christ. Sometimes, we live vicariously through others. Here is your chance to live vicariously through me. Let's delve into the next several chapters, with my testimony in mind. Indeed, a woman who has risen time and time again through Him can truly speak. Indeed, a woman who has risen over transgressions, trials and tribulations with God can relearn. First, we must learn to have our soil ready for God.

"Character cannot be developed in ease and quiet. Only through experience of trial and suffering can the soul be strengthened, ambition inspired, and success achieved."

–Helen Keller

CHAPTER 2

The Soil

Many questions plague us because much is required of us. After all, God chose us to be the bearer of life. He chose us to be His vessel to birth many into this world. I will be the first to admit that it took me years to discover the meaning of Eve's name. I wasn't always a practicing Christian woman despite being raised by Christian women. So, imagine when I found out that Eve's name actually meant life. I was deeply enthralled at the irony, that the first woman God created, he chose a name that symbolized life. Thus, we are the bearer of life which is an equal irony. Yet, some of us do not know how powerful we ultimately are. We have lost recognition of just how strong we are and can be. Just as it means to be human, we lose our way time and time again. We wander in different directions, trying to find what it is we seek.

As a child growing up, I was surrounded by strong women. I don't say this to earn good favor, but it was so evident. Growing up in New Orleans was rough in its own right. Although it is rich in culture and history, crime was just as pronounced. I will always be proud of where I am from, but happy my father created a better path for us. I would watch my grandmother, Louise, be the pillar of a God-fearing woman. She opened her home to many foster children, so that they would have life more abundantly. She would work herself tirelessly to the bone to give many a better quality of life. When I read of how Jesus fed many with just five loaves of bread and two fish, the image of my grandmother Louise appeared. She fed many with very little and impacted others with the good soil within her. My grandmother, Mary, is such a faithful servant as a Jehovah Witness, that her soil would lead many as well. My mother, Cynthia, the extension of my grandmother Louise, is in a class of her own. It is because of her, I learned to appreciate real value and not give much weight to what should not hold value. They all poured within me the seed of God that my soil must nourish. Although my actions in my adult life are questionable, the seed they planted within my soil, carried me often. It is because of their sowing I knew who I could lean on in my most difficult hour. No matter how far I strayed, I realized that seed within me was orchestrated and carefully placed.

We are used to the standard definition of Soil being the loose upper layer of the earth in which plants grow. For plants to grow strong, beautiful in its own right and stand erect, quality soil is required. The plant is the product of the seeds planted within the soil. It's beauty, its distinguishing features, and its uniqueness all lead to the soil. The Soil must be enriched with nutrients, and well taken care of. How fitting it is to speak of the soil in comparison to us as women. There is nothing more displeasing to watch than a woman who does not know the value of her soil. A woman that does not know what sustains her soil, cannot value it just as fiercely as God does or desires for her to. For the soil is a woman's heart. Jesus often spoke in parables or simple stories to illustrate morals and spiritual lessons.

His parables were not just for the times in which they were spoken, or written in a biblical sense. They represent the "forever more" and "for such a time as this". We are reminded in Chapter 13 of the book of Matthew "The Parable of the Sower". A farmer went out to plant his seed. He scattered the seed on the ground. Some fell on a path. Birds came and ate it up. Some seed fell on rocky places, where there wasn't much soil. The plants came up quickly, because the soil wasn't deep.

When the sun came up, it burned the plants. They dried up because they had no roots. Other seed fell among thorns. The thorns grew up and crowded out the plants. Still other seed fell on good soil. It produced a crop 100, 60 or 30 times more than what was planted. Those who have ears should listen and understand. As women, we must understand what Jesus meant, and how it applies to our own soils. Remember our soil is our hearts. The seeds fell upon the hard path, rocky places, thorns and good soil.

The seeds for us are all around. It is in the ability to hear and see the truth. Just as the seeds are of truth, our soils must be ready to receive them. When I look back over the actions of my life, I can honestly say I wasn't ready to face my truths. I did not have the soil necessary for the seeds to truly develop. It was my grandmothers and mother whom was doing the sowing, not of my own doing. The more they sowed, my soil was not truly ready. I thought I was a Miss Know It All at times which drove others insane--namely my mother. At a young age, you could find my vocabulary being far advanced than my physical age. Although, I was a straight A student and very seldom tested the waters, I hit the rebellious stage at 17-years-old.

Looking back, I think I hit that stage because I always walked a straight line. In high school, my peers often referred to me as Ms. McKinley rather than Merci. Perhaps it was the way I carried myself. Yet, I did not take it as a compliment. Deep down, I took it as an insult instead. Looking back, I should have taken it as them giving me the uppermost respect based on how I carried myself. Suddenly, this need to rebel just came over me. I wanted to rebel and show others, I could be their version of normal. I didn't hang out much with my friends, but I always wanted to do things for my younger siblings. It was a choice of mine, but was that really normal? Who would rather spend time with their younger siblings than go shopping or hang out at their best friend's house to gossip while growing up?

At 17, I got into a relationship with a much older guy who was 27-years-old at the time. There I was working as a cashier at Kmart, tired and having been on my feet all day. I would always make small talk with the customers that came through my line as it made the time go by faster. I was tired, hungry and in my head, counting down the minutes and seconds to my break. I looked up from closing my register and there he was, just a smiling. From the looks of it, he'd had a hard day at work himself. I tended to him as I did all my other customers. When the time came for me to get off work, I shot out of the doors of Kmart like a speeding bullet. I was trying to catch the P12 bus before it left. That day I missed the bus. I regretted having to walk two miles home after being on my feet all day. As I was getting ready to start the trek, he appeared out of nowhere asking me all kinds of questions. It wasn't long before he would know the time when I got off of work and would be there when I left Kmart. When my mother found out about him and how old he was, she forbade me to see him. I started sneaking around, disrespecting my parents and I got a little too big for my britches. The inner voice in me was saying, Merci this isn't a good idea. What are you doing? I knew it was God speaking through my conscience of right and wrong. Yet, I did not listen as my soil was not rooted in God.

One day, I made a spur of the moment decision, left without a word to my family and moved in with him. I acted without thinking. When I moved in with him, I had no idea he already had a two- year-old son. I had no idea he was looking for someone he could control or primarily do for his son. There I was attempting to play house with a person I barely even knew. I was stubborn as all get out, but I wasn't going to return home. One day, out of nowhere, I heard banging on the door. It was my mother and her neighbor from across the street–they'd driven all the way to the District of Columbia to come and get me. Low and behold, my mother, who doesn't know how to drive, had someone drive her to come and get me. It was an embarrassing scene, but she was fighting for me. I was relieved, but I didn't show it at the time. When I returned home, there was a complete silence. The great divide between my mother and I didn't need a knife at all. There were so many awkward moments as I hit a downward spiral internally. I was a long way from the little girl whom used to play church and act like a Sunday School Teacher. It was as if I saw the WARNING or CAUTION signs and still threw all caution to the wind. I was a long way from the little girl, who struggled with her self-esteem. Or was I?

Over the years, my soil became hardened without me even realizing it. My soil became hardened because of what I experienced. If our soil is hardened, the seeds cannot be properly planted. Jesus knew that some were rebellious and like hardened paths. Jesus also knew that our hearts could become hardened as we become bludgeoned by circumstance. Jesus knew that rocky places exist through the highs and lows of life. We rejoice in the fleeting moments, without processing these moments. This is why our soils must not give way to fleeting moments, for the seeds once more cannot take root. Jesus knew that we'd grow weary. He knew that we would have moments where the seeds will start to bear fruit, but soon be replaced with thorns. The thorns take shape because we grow tired and angry at the ailments that life often throws. Psalm 30:5KJV "For his anger endureth but a moment; in his favor is life: weeping may endure for a night, but joy cometh in the morning. "Just as we bear down to have children, we must constantly strive to bear down in life with our soils in favor of good. It might be a struggle to maintain that good soil, but nothing worth having ever truly comes easy. In due season, you will be proud that you endured the struggle. Good soil can bear fruit that multiply many times over.

If it had not been for my mother coming to get me during my rebellious stage, who knows where I would be. God will send us all the signs needed and through others. He will send us people whose soil is of the good seed. He will send them to pour into our own soils rooted in harden paths and thorns. Maybe we don't recognize it as such because our eyes are those of humans rather than of faith. We lose our faith in the blink of an eye. We think it is too hard for us to conform to the path of what God desires for us.

Whatever the reasons are, our faith is our lifeline. The inner struggles we face with our upbringing, past relationships or trying to be everything to everyone, tends to overshadow our faith. Our faith gets lost like it is something washed out to sea. Matthew 17:20 KJV "And Jesus said unto them, Because of your unbelief: for verily I say unto you, if ye have faith as a grain of mustard seed, ye shall say unto this mountain, remove hence to yonder place; and it shall remove; and nothing shall be impossible unto you." The smallest seed of faith can magnify in unthinkable ways. The smallest seed of faith we submit to come into our soils can lead to a bountiful harvest. A harvest requires soil, seeds, and nutrients. Our soil is that of our hearts. Our seeds are that of the word of God. Its nutrients are how we practice our faith. What is the soil of the harvest, if we don't know how to plow it? What is the soil of the woman, if she doesn't know how to deeply plow? God gives us the tools to water our harvest, and the strength to pull out its weeds. He teaches us how to deeply plow.

CHAPTER 3

Deeply Plow

B y trade, I'm not a farmer. I am not agriculturally inclined at all. We have all been in situations where we questioned if God was near. We questioned if God heard our prayers and if he had forsaken us. Deuteronomy 31:6 KJV "Be strong and courageous; don't be terrified or afraid of them. For it is the Lord thy God who goes with you; He will not leave you or forsake you." God speaks to us in many ways, but we must prepare our soil to receive. If our soil is not prepared to receive, how then can we recognize when He is speaking?

I, too, have been guilty of not cultivating my soil. There are times when I have been guilty of not recognizing God speaking to me through others or in certain situations. Perhaps, it was because I had not yet deeply plowed. How eloquent for the Lord to reference farming terms. You are a farmer, you are the harvest and you must do the plowing. We must constantly plow so we can allow God into our lives. He is always with us, but we must allow ourselves to see it. Yes, we as women are farmers too, and not similar to the farming done by men. We are farmers in a biblical sense because of the physical and spiritual labor of allowing the implantation of God's seed. Genesis 1:29 KJV "God said, "Look, I have given you every seed bearing plant on the surface of the entire earth, and every tree whose fruit contains seed. This will be for you." To the world, I interpret "deeply plow," as to modify the soil for water retention. As Christian women, we have to deeply plow our hearts to allow for the growth of God's seed. Easier said than done, right? It requires a lot of effort and hard work on our part. God reminds us in 2 Timothy that it is the hardworking famer whom has the first share of the crops. We must not stop at the first feeling(s) of resistance. Resistance also builds our strength and endurance. We have to always dig deeper, to plow deeper. As women, we are natural caregivers and nurturers yearning freely to love and be loved. I have done exactly the same, only to be met with closed fists. I know the easiest thing to do is to develop a wall, a hard exterior, and allow the thorns spoke of to overtake our soil. Jeremiah 4:3 KJV "Break up your fallow ground, and sow not among thorns."

As a veteran of our military, I traveled all over the world. I remember partying until the sun came up when I was 21 and overseas. I was not in a partying mood, but rather wanted to spend time at home in the barracks. I was known to be up all hours of the night and wee hours of the morning. As I was going to do my laundry, I saw a local national female walking out of the barracks room disheveled. From her appearance and the high fives between the males as she walked down the hall, I knew what had occurred. I looked at her and I saw the look of shame trying to be disguised by her gait. I wondered about her as I said to myself, "She could be me." I could have been her. Maybe you were her at one point in time. Maybe you knew another woman who walked "the halls of shame" or walked in the aftermath of not knowing her worth. What comes to the woman whose soil is not ready to receive God? What comes of the woman who does not know her own soil and what should strengthen it? Think of God's word as water for our soil. No other person or thing can be a substitute for that water. Our soil must bear fruit and provide nutrients for the bread of life.

The quality of what we bring forth as women depends on how well we tend the soil within us. Nothing is more disheartening than to witness a woman who constantly waters others who don't value her. Our situations can cause us to irrigate where we don't need to. We exhaust our supply and ourselves. We try to revive dead situations through the water God provided for us to invest in ourselves. Imagine if we used that very same water as we deeply plow our own soil? Jeremiah 14:4 KJV "because the ground is chapt, for there was no rain in the earth, the plowmen were ashamed, they covered their heads." God provides the water necessary, but as women equal of farmers, we expend it. We can sacrifice who we are or who we can become in the process. How must we fight as we continue to plow? We fight with an unshakeable faith and a heart filled with good and hope. 1 Corinthians 9:10 KJV "Or saith he it altogether for our sakes? For our sakes, no doubt, this is written: that he that ploweth should plow in hope; and that he that thresheth in hope should be partaker of His hope."

In my thirty-four years of existence, I cannot say it has been "a life of crystal stairs," as Langston Hughes, my favorite poet, so eloquently stated. There were times where I had to cultivate in stubborn soil. There were times I struggled not to get lost in my own understanding. Proverbs 3:5-6 KJV Trust in the Lord with all thine heart; and lean not unto thine own understanding. In all thy ways acknowledge Him and he shall direct thy paths." When I enlisted in the military, I was running with a purpose. I ran because of how I let my family down during my rebellious stage. I ran because I wanted to put myself in position to contribute something positive to my siblings' lives. Yet, when I arrived for Basic Combat Training, it was a test of true mental strength. I had not one person I could call on other than GOD. As I laid in my bunk, I often thought what have I gotten myself into?

I was always the last person in a ruck march, or the last soldier to finish a run. I was out of shape and thought about quitting. The verb "quit" was never a thought prior to this experience. Failure was not an option. Each day, I awoke and prayed to God. Every night, I prayed before climbing into my bunk. Little did I know that I was deeply plowing. It was during this time that I discovered just how many of my physical ailments would materialize. I would cry unto Him saying, "Father, I beg of you, please, do not let me fail." I was the most disciplined recruit I could possibly be, as it was instilled in me from my parents. It wasn't hard for me to conform to the standards required, but the physical regiment was far more than I could bear.

I remembered what my Grandmother Louise always said, "God will not put more on you than you can bear." 1 Corinthians 10:13 KJV "There hath no temptation taken you but such as is common to man: but God is faithful, who will not suffer you to be tempted above that ye are able; but will with the temptation also make a way to escape, that ye may be able to bear it." I would replay this in my mind as the weight of the rucksack during our Marches seemed too heavy. I was only 4 feet 9 inches tall with a 45lb rucksack on my back while marching twelve miles across uneven surfaces. It can take a toll on your body and being of short stature, it was hard. Each time I crossed the finish line of the physical fitness test, failing by seconds, this echoed in my head. It was like a never ending struggle as I often heard, "PVT McKinley, you failed again. If you don't pass we are going to send you home." I felt the sting of tears as I was trying so hard to hide behind a military exterior.

I started to think negative about myself which occurred many times over the years. The night before the final physical test, I pulled out the Bible my mother gave me in 4th grade. It was worn by the time I arrived at basic training at the tender age of 20. Instead of my turning to the usual scriptures highlighted in yellow, I was led to Psalms 40:2 KJV "He brought me up also out of a horrible pit, out of the miry clay, and set my feet upon a rock, and established my goings." I was in the pit, and it was only God that was going to bring me out. The morning came for me to take my final physical test, and I took to the track. My usual thoughts didn't exist. Instead, I thought of success. When I came across that finish line with a minute to spare, I knew it was none other than God. I plowed my hardest, but God had to take over plowing for me through the renewal of my mind. God has always given us the strength to pull out the weeds and thorns of our soil. Negative thoughts that seeped in constantly over the years were like weeds that overtook the essence of who I thought I was.

As I battled, my burdens became lighter with each moment of clarity I gained through prayer. Each time we pray, we are deeply plowing. We allow the landing of His spirit into our hearts. The times we humble ourselves before Him and turn to Him in prayer, the Holy Spirit enters our soil. God can turn a mess, into a message and a test into a testimony. Romans 12:2 KJV "And be not conformed to this world: but be ye transformed by the renewing of your mind, that ye may prove what is that good, and acceptable, and perfect, will of God." Know that God has not forsaken you and that He desires great plans in your life. We have to be willing to put in the work necessary, and remain consistent. Proverbs 12:11 KJV "He that tilleth his land shall be satisfied with bread: but he that followeth vain persons is void of understanding."

The power of intuition comes to women like lightning bolts. It is easier to get weary or become weakened by the electric shock of our intuitions. Let the shock recharge you in such a way that you become stronger. Believe in the ability of your own strength, cherish it and know its origin. It comes through our Heavenly Father as through Him, all blessings flow. Deuteronomy 11:13-15 KJV 13 "And it shall come to pass, if ye shall hearken diligently unto my commandments which I command you this day, to love the Lord your God, and to serve Him with all your heart and with all your soul. 14 That I will give you the rain of your land in his due season, the first rain and the latter rain, that thou mayest gather in thy corn, and thy wine, and thine oil." God can supply our needs. That is always His plan for us. Diligently and deeply plow your heart for Him in all seasons of your life. Each season brings forth endless possibilities for the desires of your life. Faint not as the season's change, for plowing deeply allows us to weather life's storms.

CHAPTER 4

Weather the Storms

"I have made you. I will carry you;
I will sustain you and I will rescue you."

–Isaiah 46:4

Who can better speak of weathering the storms than one who has borne many? If only we didn't live in shame of our storms, but are renewed in the midst of them.I am not supposed to be here, yet here I am before you speaking to you through written words. When I was born, I was born to a drug addicted mother, a prostitute, nonetheless. You can imagine how sickly a child I was because of it. I was placed in St. Vincent's Orphanage Home in New Orleans, Louisiana. My mother says I had the stench that comes from babies born with drugs in their system. I was premature with sunken eyes, a tiny body and a big head. Needless to say, my appearance was not pleasing to the eyes. What is so odd, is that I don't remember any of it, but I do recall my health battles thereafter.

I recall my mother telling me that before the adoption was finalized, they gave my birth mother one last chance. My mother told me of how I was at the courthouse sitting and waiting on a bench with my legs swinging and long hair in pig tails. I sat and I waited for a whole day for a woman I didn't even know existed to show up. My adoption became finalized at the age of five, but still I had not a clue I was truly adopted. All I remember were bouts with asthma, impetigo and being in and out of doctors' offices. The doctors told my mother that I would have delayed development and learning disabilities. I always felt different, but didn't know the cause of this feeling until the age of nine. I've weathered many storms, but this one came in like a hurricane that I carried internally for years. At the age of nine, my world changed with the words "You are adopted." What followed was Hurricane Norma, if that was truly her name. Norma is my birth mother's name, or so I've been told. Early on, I'd been taught to be humble in God by my grandmothers.

When I received confirmation I was adopted, my first reaction was a heart of gratitude. My second reaction was an endless stream of questions. My third reaction was a sense of abandonment. That sense of abandonment would follow me well into adulthood. Sometimes, we keep ourselves in the storms far longer than we have to. We create our own storms through unexpressed feelings we try to hide. I couldn't quite understand how a woman can carry a child, birth that very same child, and desert her in her first moments of life. I carried these burdens and thoughts like a mental weight. My Grandmother Louise often sang hymns as she cooked. One of her favorites was "Thank You" by Walter Hawkins as she prepared my favorite macaroni and cheese. When my thoughts traveled to a dark place, I mentally revived myself with those lyrics.

As I sat and thought of my biological mother and siblings, I wondered if they were alive. I know many children born into the foster care system and aged out of the system as broken adults. They never felt they were loved. God did not allow me to be one of them, but I still don't know if my siblings met a similar path. One thing I do know is God never promised us a life without trials and tribulations.

James 1:12 KJV "Blessed is the man that endureth temptation: for when he is tried, he shall receive the crown of life, which the Lord hath promised to them that love Him." I know God has never, nor will he ever forsake you. I bear witness to His unconditional love because the times I did not love myself, it was God's love for me that sustained me. If we can see past our storms and fight for moments of clarity through prayer, then we can weather storms.

The question is not always "Why?" The answers sometimes come in "How?" I've battled a sense of abandonment, struggles with self-love, domestic violence, physical ailments, and loss of comrades within the military. If you can name it, I've probably been through it. I had times when I woke up to the same tears I'd shed the previous night. I sat motionless, staring at the four walls, mentally paralyzed. I was too embarrassed to share those moments with anyone for fear of judgment. We place too much emphasis on others' perception of us, as if their opinions matter. We seek validation in those just as human and broken as we are, if not more. I remember shouting to the mirror, "Lord, please, fight for me because I can't do this by myself." It took all the strength I had to be able to speak those words.

If we speak the words that our hearts yearn to speak and call unto Him, He will hear us. Psalm 34:18 NIV "The LORD is close to the brokenhearted and saves those who are crushed in spirit." To weather the storms is to pray and allow him to enter into our soil. We must have faith in him. It is hard not to grow weary in the midst of weathering the storms because of expectations. I have been guilty of expecting immediate answers to prayers. The seeds you sow into your faith and into your soils will allow you to be able to see the answers He is providing you. Isaiah 65:24 NIV "Before they call I will answer; while they are still speaking I will hear." In our storms, we must admit our hard truths, and be transparent with ourselves and those around us. The storms continue to magnify when we run from the truths before us. As women, we have to understand no matter how far we attempt to run from those truths, the truths will always be within us.

They will remain until we decide to release it, or them, depending on the number of your truths. You can't experience true release until you give a voice to what your mind and heart need to speak. Releasing those truths allows us to also break the burdens placed upon us by ourselves or others. Prayer without faith and belief within your heart are meaningless words. Psalms 37:4-5 NIV "4 Take delight in the Lord, and he will give you the desires of your heart. 5 Commit your way to the Lord; trust in Him, and he will do this." Prayers without work are also dead. James 2:17 NIV "In the same way, faith by itself, if it is not accompanied by action, is dead." Weathering storms requires a call to action that we move and take each step of faith. Continue to pray non-stop. 1 Thessalonians 5:17 NIV says "pray continually," reminding us of such.

Stand and boldly tell your storm how big your God is. Nothing is too big for our all-powerful God. The minute you let the storm take your faith is the minute hope is lost. God does not want you to be hopeless, but filled with promise. Romans 5:2-5 ESV "Through Him we have also obtained access by faith into this grace in which we stand, and we rejoice in hope of the glory of God. More than that, we rejoice in our sufferings, knowing that suffering produces endurance, and endurance produces character, and character produces hope, and hope does not put us to shame, because God's love has been poured into our hearts through the Holy Spirit who has been given to us." I say these things because storms can sometimes hinder us from living life, becoming paralyzed in analysis or fear.

There is nothing more tragic than to be allowed to have a life, but to not truly live. Trials and tribulations are a part of life, but God is never absent during them. John 16:33 NIV "I have told you these things, so that in me you may have peace. In this world you will have trouble. But take heart! I have overcome the world." The common factor of my trials and tribulations is prayer. Should one give ear to His words through scripture, you will see He is there regardless of our circumstances.

"What matters most is how well you walk through the fire."

–Charles Bukowski

CHAPTER 5

Protect Thy Harvest

As a little girl growing up, I didn't always like to share. Since my cousin, Nettie, and I were the same age, we often received the same things. Our parents always wanted to dress us alike, for some odd reason, but we each had our own personalities. Because of that, my cousin and I had a relationship similar to sibling rivalry. You can just imagine when we received different toys or clothes from the other, we argued or fought over them, each of us laying claim to the items in question. You could always find our grandmother hollering at us to stop the bickering when all the grandkids got together.

I'd think of ways to trip my cousin up, walking to church in our "Sunday Best" with our names on our hair bows. If you grew up in the South, you could only imagine we were decked out in well-kempt threads. Once, I attempted to get my cousin into trouble just being petty and giving into the rivalry. While my grandmother was putting a hot comb to my hair, she said "Merci, God doesn't like ugly." I never understood that phrase until I got older. She made sure we all knew Galatians 6:7 KJV "Be not deceived; God is not mocked: for whatsoever a man soweth, that shall he also reap." Protecting your Harvest comes with what you sew into it. Sometimes the way in which my grandmothers spoke put the fear of God within me. For this purpose, Galatians 6:7 KJV is not referenced to evoke fear, but understanding.

The word "Harvest" can be defined in similar ways, from both the Webster dictionaries and scripture. What we plant within ourselves, its source, and how we choose to plant it, leads to our Harvest. The reaping of what is sown also leads to the livelihood and quality of that same Harvest. Thus, providing a way to protecting our Harvest within us. Growing up, I wore many hats to cover what I lacked inside. You could find me earning straight A's in school or what many would call being an overachiever.

Underneath that disguise was a young girl who struggled with self-esteem. Oddly enough, in school, I wasn't picked on for being the nerd. I wasn't a part of any clique, but got along with any and everybody. Lucky me, or was it divine intervention? Each time I thought I was building my self-esteem, it quickly escaped inside the thoughts floating within my mind. Deep down, I always knew it was because of being adopted. Even before my parents told me at the age of nine, I already knew. I always felt different or like the sore thumb that stuck out. When my parents confirmed I was adopted, it was like the floodgates of negative thoughts were opened.

I became consumed with these thoughts, often struggling with self-love and understanding what self-worth meant. This led to poor choices. I didn't quite understand that what we pour into ourselves is what builds our Harvest. I didn't quite understand that our thoughts are only a fraction of the seeds used for our Harvest. By now, you can only guess what the other half of those seeds ultimately are--our actions. Our seeds for our Harvest are a combination of our thoughts and our actions. Although my grandmothers made sure the seeds of Christian faith were imbedded, my thoughts and actions changed the quality of those seeds. I continued to excel in school, earning all kinds of accolades. When I got older and left the nest, the quality of those seeds became almost non-existent as I tried to fit in. Through God, we can protect our Harvest.

Not building my self-worth and exercising self-love led to actions I am not proud of. We must acknowledge the poor choices we make, for living in denial only magnifies them. You are worthy of being transparent and honest with yourself. Making poor choices is often a part of life. Just because you've made poor choices before doesn't mean you can't make the right ones thereafter. You must first acknowledge the poor choices for what they were to create the better choices that must follow. The quality of your Harvest and where it ultimately lies depends on it.

In life, we experience unpredicted battles. These very same battles, as often as we denied them, were sometimes before us in plain sight. Although I never cared for math growing up, the simplicity of addition and subtraction is relevant in other ways. God provides us additions necessary to increase our Harvest. He will also perform necessary subtractions to protect the Harvest He desires for us. Subtractions have to happen in order to make room for the additions and growth of our Harvest. We usually fight those subtractions, not realizing that deletion is for our protection.

My thoughts caused me to rebel against the seeds planted within me by my parentage. Proverbs 4:20-23 CEV 20 "My child, listen carefully to everything I say. 21 Don't forget a single word, but think about it all. 22 Knowing these teachings will mean true life and good health for you. 23 Carefully guard your thoughts because they are the source of true life." Our thoughts are the basic, intangible fabric of who we are. The quality of that fabric can bear all things, if we only recognize that God is the needle that crafts that fabric.

I was lost in many situations because of the way I mentally processed and evaluated my circumstances. It took me years to understand that our thoughts are the author of our worth. We must learn to write our worth, and not have someone else become the author of it. Our faith lays the foundation, thus, His word is a part of authoring our thoughts. As we experience life, we must determine who, ultimately, is the author of our self-worth. We must learn how to get back to the basics. The basics of loving who we are. The basics of valuing who we are. The basics of knowing who we are. For it is knowing the basics that leads us to what we deserve. A person is less valuable to another when they have little or no knowledge of their self-worth. Building your value in God, with God, and seeing it with the same way as He sees your value, brings the necessary. It is in the necessary, the guard and protective barrier will emerge. It is up to you to listen and make the choice.

The basics can always be reshaped with our eyes and heart cast upon the Lord himself. A heart in submission to God, with eyes open to discernment, can lead to being reshaped. For some, including me, we once surrounded ourselves with people that meant us more harm than good. God blesses us with the gift of discernment, the ability to see false intentions before us or people who have hidden agendas and harmful motives. Hebrews 4:12 KJV "For the word of God is quick, and powerful, and sharper than any two edged sword, piercing even to the dividing asunder of soul and spirit, and of the joints and marrow, and is a discerner of the thoughts and intents of the heart". To utilize this, we must stay close to the word of God. Feeding our faith with His word causes our self-doubts to perish. We are born into this life, but we must allow ourselves to be born again through the word of God. A woman rebirthed in the spirit of the Lord is a woman of wisdom and distinct virtue. This lends to the very heart of our Harvest.

Once wayward, I can say rebirth is possible. Something must internally die, in order for what yearns to rise. We must pay attention to what the Lord reveals, at times, repeatedly through others and life's circumstances. During my transient military history, someone was always inviting me to church. I didn't know if I exuded the "invite-me-to-church" aura, but it was often extended. My attendance at church was sporadic, at best. If my grandmothers knew this, how disappointed they would have been. Growing up, it was a "must" to be in church. I knew these frequent invites were God's way of saying, "Merci, my wayward daughter, come to me." He beckoned me to become reborn through Him. He was summoning me towards Him, for my hunger within could never be fed where I searched. Seeking to quench of our thirst and fulfill our hunger in the world can cause us to miss our Harvest altogether.

I was called towards baptism while serving in Iraq, but not before a certain experience. While on a convoy mission in the middle of Sadr City with the military police, our convoy halted. This required me to dismount and lay the grounds for security. While standing and pulling security, a group of Iraqi women walked by, giving me a thumbs up. They were proud to see me among uniformed male soldiers. I noticed one of the women was a part of the cleaning crew for our military base's bathrooms. At this moment, I saw her with her young child. She started pushing her child towards me and said, "Here you take to America and give good life". Just a few days later, this woman and the rest were killed. I experienced many losses during this deployment. I've experienced the loss of my comrades and friends. These very same losses led to my call towards accepting Jesus Christ as my Lord and Savior. John 11:25 NIV "I am the resurrection and the life. The one who believes in me will live" I was baptized on July 10, 2015, but was still not in full submission. Submitting to God provides the foundation to not only build our Harvest but strengthen it as well.

Protecting one's Harvest includes filtering our thoughts, and embracing God's gift of discernment. Sometimes we don't see discernment as a gift. We would rather run from it because it would mean facing truths. Yet, God continues to give us the courage for our eyes to remain open. He provides us the strength in Him, to face the pain we rather not see. Discernment only comes from growth through His word.

It is one of the many ways he provides for us. It is one of the many ways he pours His unconditional love unto us. Over the course of my military service, I lost that ability. I had not yet dealt with my sense of abandonment from my biological mother, and other issues. I didn't recognize the full amount of my own Harvest. If we don't understand the fullness of our Harvest, how can we better protect it? I carried hurt and pain, but masked it. That served no purpose and allowed toxicity to seep into my life. Protecting our Harvest is a matter of understanding, acknowledging and accepting the virtue of patience. Securing your Harvest is just one part. We must also nurture the seed of God within our soil, not letting contaminants enter. Our thoughts and choices, even friends or associates we choose for ourselves, are always a part of the equation. 1 Corinthians 15:33 NIV "Do not be misled: Bad company corrupts good character." What we contribute into our Harvest protects it; what we reap from it gives a long lasting barrier. After all, our Harvest is a representation and extension of us, deeply interwoven into our being. To fully protect it, we must have a deeper understanding of love. We must love ourselves as God loves us.

CHAPTER 6

Love Thy Self as God Loves You

Love is just as much an action as it is an emotion. God's love is selfless and unconditional. Who can better teach us of how to love, than God, who gave "His only begotten Son" for us? Who can better teach us how to love than Christ Jesus, who sacrificed himself for us? I'm not afraid to admit that I struggled to love myself, or determine my worth. Regarding my testimony, a judgment could be made that I am not qualified to ask you to love yourself. I urge you to love yourself and strengthen your worth. Let the love you have for yourself be not worldly, but spiritually balanced. Worldly love has conditions and limitations. When you fail to meet them, love is fleeting. When you love yourself with a worldly love, you encounter others' counterfeit love, to the extent of their own pleasures. Jesus loves us enough that He feeds both spiritual and physical needs. You are worthy of real and true love. Through God you are loved unconditionally with a true love.

As women, we have endured extreme hardships undergirded by love. The power of love still prompts others to rise against imposing challenges, tackling what appear to be insurmountable odds. Love is paramount because God commanded us to love. 1 John 4:7-8 7 "Dear friends, let us love one another, for love comes from God. Everyone who loves has been born of God and knows God. 8 Whoever does not love does not know God, because God is love." It's important for us to know that God will never stop loving us. God's love for us remains constant and unchanging; it simply doesn't fail. God continually pours out His love upon our lives. His love for us isn't dependent upon what we are, but who He is. How do we not know how to love ourselves? Let His love for you determine your worth. Let His love for you be that which is reflected when you look in the mirror.

I have been through moments where I let others determine my alleged value. Through being born again, I've learned that no man should have that much power. No man has that much power, unless you give him that power not knowing how to love yourself. No man should have that much influence because God's love for you is sufficient. Christ teaches us that love is the clearest mark of a Christian. As Christian women, we are growing in love and in Christ if we don't allow our past transgressions and relationships to steal this love from us. If we strengthen our love for ourselves through Him, then we know how to give and receive love.

Let your hearts be not weary of past or present burdens. Let your self-love be built on the pillars of God's word. As Christian women, the Harvest he envisions for us can only be through that of love. It is His love that allows us to be made whole. The wholeness made by God is what is needed. Ephesians 3:17-18 NLT "Your roots will grow down into God's love and keep you strong. And may you have the power to understand, as all God's people should, how wide, how long, how high, and how deep His love really is." Discover the breadth of God's love. Believe that Jesus came to redeem you. If you keep exploring His word, you will be carried to the heights which He intends to bring you.

No one lies outside the boundaries of God's love. He showed us, sending us His very best to die for our sins. Jesus died for the ungodly, not for the worthy. He died for us when we are yet sinners, not saints. He willingly went to the cross while we were still in open rebellion against Him, still coming short of His glory, still missing the mark. Yet, God manifested His love for us by allowing His son to die for us.

Jesus loves us with a love that defies human understanding. Ephesians 3:19 NIV "and to know this love that surpasses knowledge that you may be filled to the measure of all the fullness of God." He sees the very best in us, even when we can't see it ourselves. He gives us His word to maintain in all aspects of our lives, and within our hearts.

As Christian women, we probably imagine that God must feel disgusted, disappointed or discouraged with us. This can sometimes influence how we see and love ourselves. Jesus Christ's love is unyielding and relentless. He expresses love throughout His commandments. John 15:17 NIV "This is my command: love each other." Romans 13:8 NIV "Let no debt remain outstanding, except the continuing debt to love one another, for whoever loves others has fulfilled the law." Don't forget to love yourself as He is commanding us to love all. You always have been, and always will be, a part of the all. Loving ourselves as God loves us, allows us to continue to rise. The only way to continue to rise is to truly understand the power of prayer.

CHAPTER 7

Power of Prayer

"For though we live in the world, we do not wage war as the world does. The weapons we fight with are not the weapons of the world."

–2 Corinthians 10:3 NIV

Have you ever found yourself filled with negative thoughts about yourself or your situations? Have you ever found yourself not truly knowing how to pray because of it? As Christian women, we occasionally think the length of our prayers gives our prayers the power we desire them to have. God hears all prayers regardless of their length, by those who pray with a humble heart. Having a humble heart does not make us weak, or suggestive of low self-esteem. Having a humble heart allows us to go to Him as we are, faults and all, ready to seek and receive guidance. Who better to give unto us our needs through prayer than God, who accepts us as we are? The Harvest I referred to by the Bible and myself is fought and earned through prayers within God's will.

The power of prayer can change things. It can speak into any situation. It can restore hope in all the living. It can give you understanding in all trials and tribulations. The power of prayer can awaken the Holy Spirit that is planted within your soil, your heart. There is most certainly power in the ability to pray. It allows you to be restored and redeemed by God himself, not through the validation of others we desperately seek. We carry troubles within our hearts, and we don't know how to release their burden. Sometimes, our burdens weigh us down in such a way that we cease the desire, or the will to pray.

Isaiah 46:4 NIV "Even to your old age and gray hairs, I am he, I am he who will sustain you. I have made you and I will carry you; I will sustain you and I will rescue you." God is always there to release your burdens. Jesus Christ died on the cross so that we may have eternal life, and life more abundantly. If he sacrificed himself for all of us, he surely can release your burdens through prayer. Prayer gives us clarity, wisdom, and strength in our journey of life. We must never stop praying, or allow anything or anyone to take this desire from us. Prayer gives us a sense of direction that only God can provide. When we pray with hope and not doubt, we are truly praying.

When we pray in faith and not with uncertainty, we are truly placing our prayers before God. Even when there is a delay in your prayers, he is still answering your prayers. We only need to pay attention, and pray with purpose. Praying with purpose allows us to pray with the faith that is in our hearts. When we pray with purpose, we know that God gives us the answers that are beneficial to us. The power of prayer can give us favor over our enemies, and not be reduced by our circumstances. The power of prayer allows us to take on the armor of God that is needed at all times in our spiritual walk. Pray for that armor in God as we are called to do.

Ephesians 6:10-20 KJV 10 "Finally, my brethren, be strong in the Lord, and in the power of His might. 11 Put on the whole armor of God, that ye may be able to stand against the wiles of the devil. 12 For we wrestle not against flesh and blood, but against principalities, against powers, against the rulers of the darkness of this world, against spiritual wickedness in high places. 13 Wherefore take unto you the whole armor of God, that ye may be able to withstand in the evil day, and having done all, to stand. 14 Stand therefore, having your loins girt about with truth, and having on the breastplate of righteousness; 15 And your feet shod with the preparation of the gospel of peace; 16 Above all, taking the shield of faith, wherewith ye shall be able to quench all the fiery darts of the wicked. 17 And take the helmet of salvation, and the sword of the Spirit, which is the word of God: 18 Praying always with all prayer and supplication in the Spirit, and watching thereunto with all perseverance and supplication for all saints; 19 And for me, that utterance may be given unto me, that I may open my mouth boldly, to make known the mystery of the gospel, 20 For which I am an ambassador in bonds: that therein I may speak boldly, as I ought to speak."

I can't guarantee you many things, but one thing that is promised is God hears all who come to Him through prayer. God is faithful to us. If we remain persistent in prayer, filled with thanksgiving, in faith and within the will of God, the power of prayer lives forever. The power of prayer also provides us with understanding of the power of forgiveness. Oftentimes what keeps us weighted down, is our inability to forgive. We were not meant to live weighted down, but rather free of these chains. Those chains consume us in more ways than we realize. These very chains are conceived within our inability to forgive ourselves and others. The ultimate test can only be won through understanding the power of forgiveness.

CHAPTER 8

The Power of Forgiveness

"Never forget the three powerful resources you always have available to you: love, prayer, and forgiveness."

–H. Jackson Brown, Jr.

I've had many transgressions committed against me by others. With all the seeds poured into me by my grandmothers, one would think my list of transgressions would be short. Yet, it wasn't because hurt people tend to hurt others. Throughout the years, I made others pay for transgressions against me committed by people they didn't know. It was not intentional but merely how I was coping, or the lack thereof. It created a wall and a hard exterior. I've heard many speak of the liberation and power that forgiveness brings. In my quest for such, I would pray prematurely. God knows our hearts, even before we verbalize their content or intentions. My premature prayers of forgiveness were met with an unsettled heart.

The key to our Harvest is the ability to forgive, and create room to be fulfilled with abundance. I used to be bothered by the words, "Let go." I was so bothered because every time someone spoke those words, I thought they were minimizing what I've been through. Through God, I've realized that sometimes we hurt ourselves more by holding onto the hurt. We inflict more pain in the refusal of letting go. How can you truly let go? It wasn't until I became relentless in prayer that I started to forgive. I faced hard truths that God placed before me.

The Harvest I speak so much of is one of a life made whole. In its eloquence, "before one can be set free in truth, one must figure out the lie in which they are being held captive." The same sentiments that can be expressed here are made whole by virtue of forgiveness. Before we can be made whole, we must first understand which transgression, not yet forgiven, is holding us captive. Forgiveness is a conscious gift we chose to give to ourselves, and to others. My approach towards forgiveness was all wrong. I thought it was a fleeting moment through prayer. I thought it a finite moment, being filled with the Holy Spirit. We all have heard "I can forgive, but I will never forget." Instead, forgiveness is an ongoing process. We are often held captive without us truly understanding that we are. We are held captive to experiences that deprive us of becoming anew. II Corinthians 5:17 KJV "Therefore, if any man be in Christ, he is a new creature: old things have passed away; behold, all things are become new." What keeps us from truly understanding this, is not wanting or knowing how to forgive. We get lost in the storms of life. Matthew 5:45 KJV "That ye may be the children of your Father which is in heaven: for the maketh His sun to rise on the evil and on the good, and sendeth rain on the just and on the unjust."

The rain falls on all of us throughout the seasons of life. A hard-earned sense of peace is fought for on our knees through prayer. A life of abundance is fought for through our ability to forgive. Forgiveness comes through God's word. For it to come through Him, our soil must be ready to receive. A heart filled with an inability to forgive has no room for God. The power of God and His manifestations cannot dwell in a heart consumed with un-forgiveness. Our faith cannot grow within a mind that is fed with negativity. An inability to forgive brings toxicity within our thoughts.

Psalm 139:23-24 NIV "23 Search me, God, and know my heart; test me and know my anxious thoughts. 24 See if there is any offensive way in me, and lead me in the way everlasting." No one's sin is greater than the other's sin. There is a reward in seeking the high road. Attempting to hurt others that have hurt us keeps us captive in a vicious circle. The ensuing bitterness within us prevents our living life more abundantly. It prevents our Harvest from taking shape within us and before us. It becomes a part of the thorns that take roots within our hearts. Romans 12:19 NIV "Do not take revenge, my friends, but leave room for God's wrath, for it is written: 'It is mine to avenge; I will repay,' says the Lord." In the end forgiveness given through compassion sustains our bread of life through Christ Jesus. Ephesians 4:32 NIV "Be kind and compassionate to one another, forgiving each other, just as in Christ God forgave you." If God can provide us with forgiveness through the Sinner's Prayer and that of repentance, we have it within us. I do not speak as though it's easy, but I speak rather as it is necessary. Can you imagine each step you take, becoming more difficult than the last one? This is what it's like to walk along a path with not being able to forgive. I questioned God so often in my desire to forgive. The biggest hurdle was learning to forgive myself. Through the journey of forgiveness, we adapt a new way of thinking. Part of this journey is having the courage to keep our eyes open. Some of it is painful, to say the least, but worth it.

They say the mark of maturity comes from trying to understand someone who has wronged you. I forgave my biological mother for her actions. She was not prepared for motherhood. I often wondered what led her to a life of prostitution and drug use. The greatest love we can show is sometimes through our ability to walk away. If we have not within ourselves to give what a person is deserving of, it is best to walk away. Her walking away gave me a chance at life. I forgave a family member for molesting me, as only a person mentally ill could do what he did. I still can't offer any rationale for the actions of the soldiers who sexually assaulted me. I still forgave, as I fought for my sense of sanity and sense of peace. Only the power of God could have led me to this deeper understanding. The last two people I had to forgive required the deepest understanding; my abuser and myself.

As I sat in the office of a licensed clinical social worker trying to find the words to express my pain, the clinical psychologist asked many questions I did not want to answer; a horrible truth pierced my heart. For quite a bit of our sessions, I sat motionless and mute. I suppose she thought my silence was indignation. She said, "I have nothing but time. For this to work, you have to speak." Deep within, I was trying to search for the answers. I silently prayed as I sought answers to the questions. The tears flowed. It was embarrassing to disclose how I met my abuser, and the events of almost a decade to see him for what he truly was. It was embarrassing to admit publicly I never truly learned to love myself. Nor did I heed the warning signs that pointed to the truth of his true nature and our relationship.

I desperately wanted answers. What led to forgiving my abuser was when the psychologist asked me if I knew what narcissistic abuse was? I excused myself to go the restroom and I immediately took to Google to learn what it was. When I returned, we discussed it in grave detail. Forgiveness did not come easy, but it came with understanding of what he truly was. We must not constantly repaint the same canvas once the true colors are shown. I did not know that, over the years, I was being groomed for this form of abuse with his random entrances into my life. In our final session, the psychologist asked me if I was proud of myself. I felt this question was rather odd, but she wanted me to hear my answer. I could tell because her technique was to ask me to repeat certain things so I could hear myself and what I was saying.

This final session led to the road of my self-forgiveness. I could not answer the question quite honestly, but she chose to answer it for me. I could tell she was being sincere and not trying to pacify me. She wanted me to see she was proud of me. "The fact that you experienced so much in your life, but you are still here fighting, speaks volumes to who you ultimately are as a person," she said. My psychologist noted that if you still care and give unto others when you have every reason not to, it's worth being proud of. I thought of our last session, as I needed to continue to forgive myself.

My harsh truths were what I allowed from others. My harsh truths came in moments of clarity with God and in those harsh truths, I was able to forgive. I had to forgive myself for what I ultimately allowed. I had to forgive myself for not wanting to see the signs God was placing before me. Everything I was attempting to build with my abuser, was torn down brick by brick. It was God tearing it down brick by brick. God has a way of doing that in our lives because he wants better for us. He constantly redirects us, if we learn to yield rather than fight against it. I developed this understanding, to forgive myself.

Choose life, choose your Harvest, and choose God. Each time you make the effort to forgive, you are birthing a new life. Each time you put in the work to forgive, your Harvest grows. Each time you forgive, you are allowing Him to do marvelous works within your life. I sincerely desire the freedom that comes with the power of forgiveness for you, as a woman of Christian faith. The transformation is astounding, and you become worthy of a Harvest full of abundance and a sense of peace. You are worthy of all that and more. Right now, in this moment, invest in the gift of forgiveness. Where the Harvest ultimately lies first requires the power of forgiveness.

Where the Harvest lies requires a deeper understanding of the power of God's love.

"Bear with each other and forgive one another if any of you has a grievance against someone. Forgive as the Lord forgave you."

–Colossians 3:13 NIV

CHAPTER 9

Power of God's Love

We all desire love, but not just any kind of love. We desire a love based in truth and soul fulfilling love. We travel near and far, often sacrificing who we are, to achieve it. God's love is every bit as enduring as it is everlasting. God's love is based in truth and it is soul fulfilling. He sacrificed His only begotten Son, Jesus Christ, for us. He sacrificed His Son to show us the truth, the way and the light. He provided us with truth in Him. Thus, birthing discernment as we travel trials and tribulations. He provided the way with His word in biblical scripture, giving us the strength to make it through many storms. He provided us with the light, giving us the gift of faith.

How many times have we sought others only to face disappointment? How many times have we looked to others and ended up having to quench a counterfeit love? A counterfeit love based upon conditions. Love based upon expectations. Love that disappears when conditions and expectations are not met. We call many, but few answer. We turn to others, but few deliver. Yet, when we call unto the Lord, he is there. When we turn to Him, he delivers. We think our way out of His love for us. We allow our past transgressions to consume us so much that we doubt His love for us. When Jesus Christ was brought to the cross, He was mocked, bludgeoned and adorned with a crown of thorns. Can you see Him? Can you see His blood, His tears, His pain? Even in this moment, he said "forgive them father for they know not what they do".

Even in this moment, he thought about us. Even in this moment he displayed so much love for us through His son.

Many times, I turned to Him. There has not been one time where He was not there. I asked God to fight for me, and that He did. I asked God to give me purpose, and that he did. I asked God to not give up on me. He not only answered, but he called me to deliver the Harvest. Only God's love for me can allow me to rise over tragedy. Only God's love for me can allow me to walk with my head held high rather than hung in shame. The same shame that many would want me to perish within. I've experienced my greatest hurts thus far, but in His love, I received the capacity of me. I distinctly remember the aftermath of my sexual assault in the military. Many in my unit avoided me as though I was diseased. No one talked to me and many shunned me. I had not one person I could turn to. Yet, God was there to deliver me from the bathroom in which I contemplated ending my life. Years later, I would be faced with the same circumstance only to have my abuser laugh as he struck me with his fists. He kicked me repeatedly, gloating in his sadistic power. The echoes of his laughter lived inside of me long after the bruises had healed. The echoes of his laughter inside my head led me to ask God to allow me to come home.

God allowed me to reclaim Merci and fight for my military career. It was His love for me that allowed me to make it through. It is true that His love will allow you favor over your enemies. It was His love alone that allowed myself to reclaim my career in the same unit that ostracized me after my sexual assault. It was His love that sent me my former First Sergeant to deliver me from the same bathroom in which I contemplated suicide. I contemplated suicide because my mind could not fully process my sexual trauma. I was paraded around in hospital scrubs in front of my entire battalion of strangers, yet Soldiers and comrades. I was talked about constantly, shunned, and met with disdain over people's opinions and judgements. Yet though they doubted and mocked me, God allowed me to earn ranks and promotions within that same unit. He allowed me to grow from a victim, to a Survivor, and the voice of future Survivors as a Victim Advocate within the military.

It was His love alone that nourished my broken soul which was tormented from the abuse and mockery of my abuser. It was His love that spared my life during military deployments, and from the hands of my abuser. It must have been very disappointing for God to hear me plead with Him to allow me to come home to be with Him. I was lost, I was broken, I was simply a shell of a person. It was God's love and His alone that rescued and revived me. Only the power of God's love can accomplish this and not that of man. Only God's love could have mended my broken pieces to steadily rise with His love as the foundation of my strength.

Never doubt the power and extent of God's love for you. There is no greater love. There is no other love that can restore you and redeem you. His unconditional love, full of Grace and Mercy, is the most precious there is. He tells us time and time again. He has not, nor will he ever forsake you. He answers us not with what we want, but with what we need. He cares so much for us that he constantly provides for us even when we don't live according to His word. His love cannot be contained inside the human mind. It is a mind and heart based within the spiritual seed, that can see the power of His love. We question God in so many moments of our lives. Yet though we question Him, he is steadfast and loyal to us. His love is breathtakingly beautiful.

His love is ever lasting, and though we sin, he is constantly there to help us along our path. He leads us to the powerful water that nourishes our soul. He leads us to the bread of life that sustains us beyond any circumstance. The power of His love, shows us the way to our Harvest. His love leads us to where our Harvest ultimately lies.

CHAPTER 10

Where The Harvest Lies

Your Harvest may not always be tangible. Sometimes, your Harvest is planted within you while you are doing the sowing. Sometimes your Harvest is in the person you constantly mature into becoming. Don't be discouraged, for it is already being manifested where it was intended to grow. Your Harvest is given through the Blood of Jesus Christ. A woman who understands where her Harvest lies and its origin can be uprooted, replanted anywhere, and survive. You can make it through the fire, and rise victorious in all aspects of life. The times you deeply plow and hold fast to your faith, you will reap an abundance that will sustain you. The determination you have in not allowing thorns and maliciousness take root in your heart will be rewarded. You will not have sown the hurt into others that was sown unto you. A deeper understanding of Job 4:8 NIV "As I have observed, those who plow evil and those who sow trouble reap it", will allow you to keep protecting your Harvest. When you love yourself as Christ does, there is a reward in self-esteem. It draws you closer to God. In God, you find unconditional love, peace, and the bread of life. There is beauty in the storms you survived.

The times when you allowed your heart to be guided by the Holy Spirit will be rewarded in ways that you could not imagine.

The fulfillment you received by being a faithful servant seeking validation and redemption in God will continue to provide you peace. The peace you gain doesn't mean that you will no longer have any trials and tribulations. It means that you will have the ability to endure those trials with the peace of knowing God still provides. You will have the peace of knowing God will always work things out for your good. The heightened sense of discernment you will gain from God's word will give you the armor needed to protect your Harvest. The Harvest that you will come to carry within will allow you to not be confined by man's judgment. Sometimes, chains are placed upon us by the judgment of others. We tend to sink deeper and deeper into the valley because of the chains shackled to us. Those chains will be broken; you will rise as the beautiful woman you rightfully are. Our beauty is not contained to our physical features, but the beauty of God's word within our hearts. After Peter's great confession of His failures, God restored Peter. God saw past His imperfections, and saw what he could be. As Christian women, he will do the same for us time and again. He will restore you the more you remain steadfast and loyal in your faith.

Patience sown into you allows an understanding of God's timing. When we lack patience, we reap consequences not intended by God. When faith serves as your compass, you can live life forward. In God, you will come to learn as I have learned, negativity cannot grow where it is not fed. If we learn to starve negativity by feeding our minds and hearts with the word of God, we are earning our Harvest. Your past will no longer have power and control over you. Thinking of our past only brings hindrance. The knowledge you carry within you can bear sustaining, spiritual fruit. Galatians 5:22-23 NIV 22 "But the fruit of the Spirit is love, joy, peace, forbearance, kindness, goodness, faithfulness, 23 gentleness and self-control. Against such things there is no law." The fruits you will bear will be marvelous as you have endured the test of time, and remained close to your faith. Your Harvest will be deeply rooted. No matter where you are replanted, you will have what it takes to thrive. Your wisdom will be astounding, and you will apply it to all facets of your life. You will cease to be morally deficient. Proverbs 3:13-18 "How blessed is the man who finds wisdom, And the man who gains understanding. 14 For her profit is better than the profit of silver, and her gain better than fine gold. 15 She is more precious than jewels; and nothing you desire compares with her. 16 Long life is in her right hand; in her left hand are riches and honor. 17 Her ways are pleasant ways, and all her paths are peace. 18 She is a tree of life to those who take hold of her, and happy are all who hold her fast."

A WRITTEN WORD

Many have asked me, "How do I survive after all the testimonies I've shared?" I say to all that with faith and God, I can survive all things. If we learn to love ourselves and each other with balanced, spiritual love and not that of the worldly love, we can become fulfilled. It took me years to learn this along my Christian walk as many times over I've experienced heartbreak and trauma. I was seeking a worldly love that yields judgment. We are not meant to be loved with a counterfeit love, but rather real love through God. Let God do the mending. Let God fight your battles. Let Go and Let God.

This judgment of the world is not for us to own. In return, if we can see ourselves with the love that God has for us, we can see ourselves for who we are and desire to become. I would like to leave you with the knowledge that in God all things are possible. You can discover the true meaning of love. In Him, you can find unconditional love, and the strength needed to face trials and tribulations with clarity. You can find peace and a Harvest filled with an abundance of wisdom, the power of forgiveness, and the true value of wealth. A woman that stands with God and in Him, truly has the wealth necessary. A woman that loves the Lord with every fiber of her being, has the wealth provided by God.

You can find your self-esteem, your worth, and your value that no man can define. In His word he faithfully tells us he is for us in Isaiah 41:10 NKJV "Fear not, for I am with you; Be not dismayed, for I am your God. I will strengthen you, yes, I will help you, I will uphold you with My righteous right hand." In His word, he tells us he loves us Jeremiah 31:3 KJV "I have loved thee with an everlasting love:

therefore, with lovingkindness have I drawn thee." When the world tells us no, he says yes through His ability to constantly provide for us. When you receive that rejection, turn to God to receive that resounding yes spoken through the Holy Spirit. Philippians 4:19 KJV "But my God shall supply all your need according to His riches in glory by Jesus Christ." When others don't believe in you, and you are having a hard time believing in yourself. God believes in you- Ephesians 3: 17-19 tells us so. When you are burdened, God says turn to Him in Matthew 11:28, and He will give you rest. When you are doubting just how strong you are and can become, allow God to give you His strength. He tells us so eloquently through Philippians 4:14 KJV. "God is always with you, and never fails unto a heart that truly believes. Allow Him into your hearts, where the true seed of faith can grow. You can and will become empowered along all walks of life. You will be fulfilled in the bread of life that will sustain you.

Cherish your walk in your Christian faith and continue to grow and become the beacon of light unto darkness of many. We are women and daughters of the Highest, who has never forsaken His children. He never fails, as we are told through Deuteronomy 31:6 KJV "Be strong and of a good courage, fear not, nor be afraid of them: for the Lord thy God, he it is that doth go with thee; he will not fail thee, nor forsake thee." Never be broken by man, but be made whole in God. You are fiercely and wonderfully made, loved by an all-powerful God who is a Rock, Sword, and Shield. Carry this with you and nurture your seed of faith. Embrace the power of forgiveness and prayer, build on the foundation of His wisdom, and love yourself as God loves you. God often provides us with an astounding wisdom that serves as a compass in life. Many times, with this wisdom, we can be redirected. Many times, with this wisdom, we can survive.

Communicate with God so you can know Him for yourself, and protect your Harvest through a never ending prayer of thanksgiving and application of the knowledge he pours into our hearts that remains ready to receive. Carry God in your hearts and be defined through His definition of whom you ultimately are. A woman that is defined by God with a love of Him within her hearts, is a rare gift. She will be able to stand erect. She will be able to weather the storms. She will come out of each storm stronger than before. Beautiful in her own right, and truly the virtuous woman He wants us all to be.

LOOK IN THE MIRROR

Look at yourself in the mirror
With the beauty as God sees you
Look past the hurt, and past the tears
And know that God is seeing you through

Look in the mirror with a love
So fiercely and wonderfully made
Uniquely crafted from the heavenly father above
Be not weary or dismayed

Look in the mirror with faith and conviction
You are not defined by relationships that did not last
Look beyond your ailments, pain and afflictions
You are worth so much more than your past

Look at yourself with the love as God sees you
With a faith built through prayer
Beyond your fears as God is working anew
Releasing the burdens, you thought you could not bare

–Merci L. McKinley–

THY REWARD, THY CROWN

You are the daughter of the most
Fiercely valued by a heavenly father
For every need he shall supply
All the broken pieces he shall gather

Every seeds of faith planted
Believing he has not forsaken
Knowing you are never abandoned
Your adornment since birth is never taken

The paths along your journey
Your unyielding consistency
Shouting His praises and existence
Loyal to being of substance

All leads to the greater reward
Wear it proudly, in your faith, you earned your crown
It shall not be denied or ignored
Let no man have the ability to tear it down

–Merci L. McKinley–

QUESTIONS FOR THE READER

1 What moments in your life caused you to stray in your faith?

2 At this moment in time, what can you do to increase your faith?

3 Do you think discernment is one of the many gifts given to us by God?

4 Have you noticed the more your faith increases, the more wisdom you gain?

5 How can you learn to love yourself as God loves you?

6 What scriptures have you had to rely upon for clarity in your life?

7 God's love for us is sufficient, and he supplies all of our needs. How has GOD supplied and sustained you in your life?

8 What have you gained from my testimony?

ABOUT THE AUTHOR

Merci McKinley is an Author and Poet. She is a native of Prince George's County, Maryland and a Veteran of the United States Military. She hails from Excelsior College in Albany, New York with a Bachelor Degree in Social Science. Merci is a best-selling author from her contributions to "Silent No More: Camouflaged Sisters" with Lila Holley, renowned veteran and life coach. She sparks strength and healing in others through her shared testimonies and "Lyrical Interventions". She has collaborated in other book projects such as "Her Story II Project," with Certified Life Coach Stacy Bryant and" Finding Your Voice, The Strong & Assertive Woman," with renowned Linda Ellis Eastman, Life Coach and CEO of Professional Woman Publishing, LLC. She challenges others to know it is not where you started from, but where you are determined to go. The key is to not give up on yourself in between. She knows that trauma can have one just existing, rather than thriving and living. She is on a personal quest to change that by helping others reclaim their lives. To share your reviews or connect with the author, please visit www.upliftpublications.com

"We must learn to grow through what we've been through. We must learn to use that as a means to propel us forward. Trying to understand the why is not as great as learning it from the person you become after it." - Merci McKinley-

Made in the USA
Middletown, DE
01 September 2024